LAUGHTER

IS AN

INSTANT

VACATION

*A Humorous Guide
to a Positive Mindset*

BETH DODD

LAUGHTER IS AN INSTANT VACATION

A Humorous Guide to a Positive Mindset

Beth Dodd

Copyright © 2024—Reflek Publishing

For more information follow me on Instagram: @funnyysister

ISBN (paperback): 978-1-962280-45-7
ISBN (e-book): 978-1-962280-46-4

This book is dedicated to my father, Robert A. Dodd Sr., whose humor and zest for life taught me how to navigate even the rockiest seas. Dad, even though it didn't seem so, I actually was listening.

Table of Contents

Foreword

As I write this foreword, I can't believe that I've truly known Beth Dodd for over a decade. What you're about to experience in this book is an evolution of someone who is not afraid to look life in the eyes, make light of it, and, at the same time, take it by the horns no matter how much it flops her around.

My relationship with Beth has evolved over our decade of knowing one another. In there, we've mixed into our interactions candor, humor, and our love for the mind. I hope you will enjoy the simplicity and the way she describes mindsets. I also hope you will see the laughter that colors the way she sees the world and then, in the process, fall in love just like I did with her method of looking at the world even when she's terrified.

If you ask Beth, she will say she doesn't know why she chose to write a book. However, as you read on, you will understand that she was meant to write a book. What you'll find out as you read is a sprinkle of academia but mainly six decades of living life unapologetically, with some very funny stories along the way. Some might find these jokes offensive, but I guarantee that if you continue to give the book a chance, you will see that Beth understands the complexities and the wisdom of taking life moment to moment.

We all have to do it afraid. And in this book, that's exactly what Beth has done— while showing you how to get your mind on track with micro steps as you laugh along the way!

Life can be terribly complex. And yet, at times, it can be so simple. As you peruse these very matter-of-fact chapters, I expect that you will laugh and nod in agreement regarding some very well-known facts. Finally, I hope you take a few things with you to move your world in a laughing direction. I know it can be easy to tell someone to laugh. Yet, when life feels resolved to give you reasons not to laugh, you can find yourself etched in a pattern of indifference, which is even worse. Beth's intention is to share insights that her brilliant father passed along to her. She takes you on a sightseeing tour of some of the painful and embarrassing moments in her life, and she tries to show you in real time that no matter how much life told her she could not, as a true Jersey girl, she clenched her fist, pumped it in the air, and said, "I sure will, in my own time, laughing. And while I am at it, I will take a bunch of people laughing with me!"

Is that you? I sure hope so!

Enjoy your read, and laugh for and with me in the process

Bola Adelakun, LPC, ACS, NCC

Chapter 1

Laughter Is an Instant Vacation

"Laughter is an instant vacation." What a great quote! I remember my dad saying that all the time. I used to think he made it up, but if I am being honest, I believe comedian and actor Milton Berle coined it. However, unless you are ninety years old today, you probably have no idea who Milton Berle was, so I am just going to give the props to my dad. He said it all the time, and he lived his life that way.

Daddio, as I affectionately called him—or Pa, as he was known to his grandchildren—was an exceptional man. Born in 1928, he lived through the Great Depression as an only child to his parents, my grandparents. When he was fifteen years old, he developed osteomyelitis, which is inflammation of the bone caused by an infection, in his right hip. Since he was not quite done growing, it stunted the growth in his right leg, and he lived the rest of his life walking with a limp.

He once told me the story of how he was in school one day, and a girl asked him if he was going to the dance. He replied, "Why should I go? I can't dance with my leg like this." The girl replied, "Hey, Bob. Why don't you stop feeling sorry for yourself and start living your life?"

That right there was the beginning of his life. He knew she was right, and he vowed to make the best out of every situation and move forward with humor and positivity. And that he did.

Daddio was a jokester. He was always positive and funny, and he could work a room like no other. He was a salesman back when salesmen were out on the road. There were no Zoom calls and no social media, so he went out there and pounded the pavement to sell his product. He was quite successful at what he did. People loved him, and he always made them smile. The global company he worked for soon recognized his wit and positivity, and they made him director of motivation. Now in his element, he could go out and inspire people with his zest for life and optimistic outlook. He traveled the world, giving motivational speeches and touching the lives of those who heard him. To this day, people share endearing stories of my dad, and most of them involve how he changed their mindset, therefore changing their lives.

After he retired, Daddio had a difficult time with his vision, so I would take him to all his doctor appointments since he could no longer drive. It was during his final five years that I actually got to really know my dad. I had heard all his sayings my whole life, such as "When life hands you lemons, make lemonade." (Of course, I took that to heart and added vodka as well . . . I'm extra like that) Another favorite was "If you didn't have bad days, you wouldn't know what good days are."

But there was something about me being a mom and listening to him as an adult. I mean *really* listening to him. It hit me differently than when I was a teenager. I started doing videos with him that I affectionately entitled "Driving with Daddio." I posted them on Facebook for fun, and he soon had a following.

The videos were only about three minutes long at most, but he sure did utilize those three minutes. He was funny and quick-witted, and at the end of every video, he would give his "profound thought" for the day. I would have a slew of comments from people he didn't even know, and, of course, I read each one to him. His face would light up because he knew he had made someone smile. After all, he thought that is why we are all here on Earth—to make each other smile. He never did get the concept of how these people were seeing the videos, but that did not stop him from spreading humor and positivity.

He passed away in November 2021. I firmly believe it was because he was ready. My mom had passed nineteen years earlier, almost to the day, and all his friends were gone as well. I think he realized the party was up in the penthouse in the sky and that it was his time to make an entrance and make the angels smile and laugh. He was ninety-three years old, and, in Daddio fashion, he kept talking about how fun and awesome his life was until he could no longer speak. People continually told me how much they missed him, his videos, and his big personality, and I thought it was a shame that so many people didn't get to enjoy him and learn from him like I did.

And then it hit me. His legacy of wisdom about the power of positivity and laughter should be available to everyone, along with tools and coping skills to give you the confidence to be who you are meant to be. All done in a simple and fun way. So . . . Ta-da! Here it is.

My book.

In the following chapters, I will share the most cherished lessons I received from my dad. Things I still use every day. Like the time he told me the first thing a guy looks at on a girl is her teeth and her nails. Yes, I believed him. Of course, we all know what they really look at, but my dentist and my manicurist are, to this day, forever in his debt. But to understand what I will share about my dad—and the wisdom he imparted to me—you will want to get to know me a little bit too. So let's start there, with the first age-old question:

Where are you from?

I'm Beth, Nice to Meet You

I'm Beth. I'm just a girl from Jersey. A Scorpio from Jersey. Double whammy right there, right? I get my humor and positivity from my dad and my tough exterior with the soft inside from my best friend, a.k.a. my mom. I am a true Jersey chick. The good. The bad. And the ugly. And I own *all* of it.

Let me explain what that means. There are people from North Jersey and people from South Jersey. We'll get into the differences in a minute, but we all have the same core values in common:

1. We are passionate about being from Jersey, whether people like it or not. If, by chance, we are out of state and meet someone from Jersey, we say, "You from Jersey? I'm from Jersey!" We find out where in Jersey they are from, have a short conversation, and move on. No long, elaborate conversation necessary. We have established our solidarity.

2. A true Jerseyan will never say, "*New* Jersey," in conversation. It's *Jersey*. There is nothing *new* about it.

If we live here, our parents, grandparents, and great-grandparents most likely do or did as well. I think it is safe to say that very few people randomly decide to move to Jersey. The fact of the matter is you have to be born into Jerseyism. It is not a learned behavior. It's innate. You either got it or you don't.

3. We don't take shit. We will call you out if we think you are lying, and we will support you if we think you are telling the truth. We are passionate about what we believe in and how we feel. And family is everything. Don't mess with our families. Because, as I mentioned, most of our extended family is here too. And they all have the same attitudes and beliefs.

4. We vacation at the Jersey Shore. And when we do, we say we are going "down the shore." We do not say we are "going to the beach" or "going down *to* the shore." It's *down the shore*. This is serious to a Jerseyan. You say it any way other than "down the shore," and you will get a look like you just disclosed where Jimmy Hoffa is buried. Don't do it.

5. We do not pump our own gas. We are not allowed. It is against the law in our state. After living here my entire life, I would venture to say there is probably a good reason for that law. I just don't want to know what it is.

But here's a fun fact: New Jersey is actually divided into two parts. There is North Jersey, and there is South Jersey. With all those core concepts above that we share, we also have differences that would make you almost think we are two different states. Quite frankly, although there's camaraderie among us because we are all from Jersey, we know we are separate entities.

For example, we follow different sports teams. I was born and raised in South Jersey, so I am a die-hard fan of the Philadelphia sports teams: the Eagles, the Flyers, the Phillies, the 76ers. People from North Jersey follow . . . Well, who cares who they follow, right? (See what I mean?) We eat the same food, but we insist on calling them different things. For example, South Jerseyans use the term *pork roll*, while North Jerseyans call it *Taylor Ham*. What is it? It is a meat that contains lightly smoked pork, salt, preservatives, and spices. It can be served alone on the side with eggs or in a sandwich with a fried egg and cheese. And it is delicious! There has been a long-standing feud over Pork roll vs. Taylor Ham. It's the same thing. The exact same food. But yep! You guessed it. We will fight over it.

We have different accents as well. North Jerseyans sound like they have a New York influence. South Jerseyans sound like we have a Philadelphia influence. And we fight and put each other down. But we're all from Jersey, and we secretly love each other for that.

Now, there is a blurred line between North Jersey and South Jersey, and that is where Central Jerseyans reside. They just live in their mansions and laugh at both sides for their pettiness. It's a good time for all.

All joking aside, my parents were born and raised in North Jersey, and many of my cousins are from North Jersey. As I said, I was born in South Jersey, so I know both worlds. Underneath our hard exterior, we are all Jerseyans.

You might be reading this and thinking I'm describing residents of Mars. But don't fear—this isn't *Star Trek*, and while we're on the subject of TV shows, we are also nothing like the cast of *Jersey Shore* or *The Real Housewives of New Jersey*. Just do not get the misconception that we are like what you see on TV. And, of course, let's not forget *The Sopranos*.

We are not . . . Wait. Okay, well, we might be like *The Sopranos*, but we're not like the other two.

You may not be from Jersey, but I am confident that, in some ways, we are a lot alike. Maybe you're married. I was married. I had a classroom marriage. What's a classroom marriage? It's a marriage in which you learned a lot. If you ever find yourself looking back at a marriage that has ended, don't ever say you had a "failed marriage." Because you did not fail. Of course, I thought that way at first when my marriage broke up. I felt like a failure. I didn't just wave and say, "Okay, see ya! Thanks for the lessons!" No, I was mad and angry. I was embarrassed. I needed healing and encouragement that everything was going to be okay. I dove into self-help books and personal growth seminars. I got that different perspective ·that I mentioned that allowed me to take the good and release the bad. I acknowledged the lessons and moved forward. So, if you walked out of a marriage knowing what you do or do not want in a relationship, then it was a classroom marriage. You learned. You never fail. You either reached your goal or you learned. I learned in that marriage.

Also, I had jobs. I'm sure you've had jobs as well (at least one, unless you got lucky and bought that winning lottery ticket and are reading this in your vacation home in the South of France). As for me, some of my jobs worked out, and some did not. When I was twenty years old, I was a telephone operator for Western Union. It was a time before email was born, so people would send telegrams. They would call in and dictate their telegram, and we operators would type it and send it off anywhere in the world. I would often hang up on people just because I didn't like their voice or I thought they had an attitude. (Funny, I thought THEY were the ones with the attitude!) I got fired from that job. (I know, surprise, surprise. Right?)

I went to college later in life. (I find it ridiculous that we make eighteen-year-olds decide what they want to do for the rest of their lives. I *still* don't know!) But after my classroom marriage, I went to college to expand, to grow, and to learn. I had learned enough in my marriage to know that I wanted to get a degree to help other people who perhaps were in or had been in a classroom marriage. So that is what I did. I went to Rutgers University and got a degree in psychology.

I have been in abusive relationships, and maybe you've experienced this too (although I do hope that you are *unlike* me in this case). I have been in some really fun relationships as well. And I have done things I'm not proud of. Like the time I got drunk and decided to get up and sing karaoke *and* dance while doing it. Not a proud moment. (The next morning, I confidently crossed "singer" and "backup dancer for J.Lo" off my list of potential career choices.) But, of course, there are many things that are a little more serious than drunk karaoke that I am not proud of. But again, I learned and moved on.

Through all of this, I learned there is always a light at the end of the tunnel. Whether that tunnel is a marriage so dark you can't breathe or the black tunnel vision of a night that precedes the worst hangover of your life, there is always a light. If you choose to live, then you're guaranteed to get through every bad day you'll ever have. How do you know? Well, because you've already done it. You have a 100 percent accuracy record for getting through every bad day you have ever had, and you will continue to do so. No matter how bad a situation is, there is always a light at the end of the tunnel.

And I promise you, it is not an oncoming train.

Why You Need This Book

If you're trudging through life, perhaps not miserable but not exactly happy, then I feel you. I've been there too. You're stuck in the never-ending cycle of a five a.m. alarm bell, yoga, shower, drive to work, commute home, cook dinner, zone out in front of the TV, get lost in the scroll hole on your phone, go to bed, wake up, and do it all over again.

Or maybe you've received the worst news of your life. A cancer diagnosis. The death of your mom. Your dad. Your dog. Your child. You lost your job or your will to live, and you think it can't get any worse than this. But can it get better? I'm telling you, friend, that it can.

What you need is a new perspective.

You need this book.

Sometimes we get so caught up in our own shit that we cannot see the forest for the trees. At times, you need to hear it from somebody else who has been through shit just like you have been through in order to have it land a different way. Sometimes you need to be reassured that the sun will come out. Never has anybody ever had a cloudy day every day of their life. All you need are some coping skills, a little lightheartedness and laughter, and a different mindset. All you require is to learn that *you* control your mindset. When you control your mindset, you control your thoughts. When you control your thoughts, you control your emotions. When you control your emotions, you control your actions. And when your actions are controlled, you control your life.

That's where this book comes in. Together, we'll work on coping skills that will help you control what's going on in your head. I am here to help you. I consider myself a mindset mentor, not a mindset coach. What is the difference? Think of a sports coach. A sports coach will have the team run laps, teach them offensive and defensive skills, and teach them plays and drills, just to name a few. They will do these things day in and day out until it becomes second nature to the team. It becomes a process of duplication, and no matter who is in any given position on the field or the court, if they are on this coach's team, they are going to learn these skills and drills.

And this totally works. For sports teams.

Now, don't misunderstand me. I realize that a coach's responsibilities go much further than what I mentioned. Strategy, player development, and in-game management are also involved. I would never underestimate the job of a coach. However, I have found that when changing someone's mindset, drills, skills, and laps don't work. Everybody's thoughts are different.

So, when you work with a mentor, you are thinking your own thoughts. The mentor is helping you with *your own* thoughts and giving you coping skills so you can be in control of what is going on in *your* head.

I am not going to control your thoughts. *You* are going to control your thoughts. I'm just going to mentor you as to what you could possibly do to change and perhaps bring to light how you might be unconsciously sabotaging your mindset. We are all individuals with our own thoughts, circumstances, and ways of learning. You are going to do what works for *you* and what keeps *your* mind in the right place.

You have the ability to achieve happiness and joy. And, most especially, you have the ability to become the best version of yourself. Not only do you have the ability, you deserve it all.

As you are reading, I ask that you keep these core concepts in the forefront of your mind:

1. Balance: For every negative, there is a positive.
2. Personal development and a positive mindset are things you need to work on daily.
3. Whatever you expect, you are going to get.

Ready to get started?

Me too. Pack your bags. We're going on a trip!

Chapter 2

Thanks, Todd

"Don't look in the past unless you plan on going that way."

—Robert A. Dodd Sr.

My dad used to say that all the time, and from the first time I heard it, I understood what he meant. We cannot go back and change things once they have been done or said. We can only look forward and keep on going.

Can you think of something you've held on to that you couldn't seem to shake? Something that keeps you up at night or makes you talk to yourself in the shower for far too long, wondering:

Why did I say that?

Why did I do that?

What must they have thought of me?

"I should have said this instead to really put them in their place!" (That's a big one. I can't count how many arguments I have won in the shower after the fact.)

No matter the situation, I'm sure you've been there. I know I have. Like that huge mistake I made that lasted for twenty years. But unlike my shower arguments, there was no looking into the past to correct this one. Let me explain . . .

The year was 1983. Okay, so right about now, some of you Gen Zs cannot believe we even had radios back then, but we did. It wasn't that long ago, actually. I certainly wasn't riding my dinosaur to work, but I was jamming in my 1980 Chrysler Cordoba with the "fine Corinthian leather." Again, sorry, Gen Zs. You have no idea what I'm talking about.

Anyway, back in 1983, musician Todd Rundgren came out with a song that I absolutely loved. It was entitled "Bang the Drum All Day," and I sang it *everywhere*. At parties. At the mall. At home. At work. Walking into church. You get the picture. In the first line of the lyrics, Rundgren explained how he didn't want to work. He preferred to bang the drum all day.

Catchy tune it was. But I actually thought the title was "I Don't Want to Work," *not* the actual title of "Bang the Drum All Day." Stick with me. You'll understand why that is important. You see, back then, we didn't walk around with portable teleprompters (a.k.a. cell phones) that supplied us with on-the-spot information. So if we wanted to know the lyrics to a song, unless we went out and bought the album or cassette tape (I know what you are thinking, keep it to yourself), we just had to wait for the song to come on the radio to catch the next line or verse.

This brings me to my twenty-year dilemma.

I had the words very, *very* wrong. I was singing, "I don't want to work, I want to *bang on each other all day*." Yes, I honestly thought those were the words.

Now remember, I said I sang that song *everywhere*.

"I don't want to work, I want to bang on each other all day!"

Come to think of it, I had a lot of dates that year. And here I thought it was because of my vibrant personality. Now I know it was because I was singing my way to a bad reputation . . .

But seriously, imagine! Walking into church! (I wonder if those church people are still praying for me.) I didn't just sing this song. I sang it loud and proud. Of course I did. I was a Todd Rundgren fan, and that's what we did!

Fast-forward to 2006, when my lifeline and best friend, Google, was up and thriving. I was dipping my toes into the information age and enjoying the instant gratification of looking up anything I needed to know. One particular day, I was getting ready for work, and I absolutely did not want to go. I had seventy-seven other things I would have rather done on that particular day. Well, wouldn't you know it—my long-time favorite Todd Rundgren song popped into my head. I started to sing the first lyrics (*my* version), and I could not remember the next verse. So, with my phone in hand, I asked Google what the lyrics were. In amazing Google style, the lyrics appeared within seconds.

And there they were. The *actual* words. Wait . . . He wanted to bang *the drum* all day?

I could feel the blood leaving my face, and the last twenty years flashed before my eyes. I was mortified. I recounted every single place I could remember where I sang that song. I could not believe it. I sat down and stared silently for about twenty minutes, which, trust me, is an eternity when you are all of a sudden residing in Humiliation Town. All kinds of thoughts went firing through my head simultaneously.

They're all laughing at me.

They must think I'm sex crazed.

They're talking about me right now.

It was excruciating. I put myself through twenty minutes of self-induced hell. And when they were over, I actually began to laugh. *Really* laugh. So much so that I was sad that there was no one there to share it with me . . .

I realized two things then.

1. I really did not like being wrong.
2. Literally nobody cared.

You Don't Have to (Always) Be Right

I felt embarrassed that I had been singing those song lyrics wrong for twenty years. But I think another thing I felt was shame . . . not over singing about wanting to bang all day, but simply because I realized I was wrong. And as a woman and a human, I dearly love to be right. In fact, humans have the need to be right. Have you ever been with somebody who made you feel like you just could not do anything right? They were right about everything? I mean, it's okay to have your opinion, but even a broken clock is right twice a day.

People have the need to be right for a few reasons. It is mostly based on fear, uncertainty, and our desire to feel connected to each other. It subconsciously covers up any feelings we might have of inadequacy or failure while elevating our self-image. It gives a false sense of instant gratification and validation, as well as a sense of belonging with those who agree with us. When you obtain this sense of gratification or validation, your brain's reward center releases dopamine, which gives you that "feel-good" response, whether it is warranted or not.

The Center of the Universe

You see, humans can be very egocentric, meaning we think everything revolves around us as individuals. When faced with conflict, embarrassment, or even a Black Friday shopping experience, in that fleeting moment, we have regard only for ourselves. As harsh as it sounds, others just do not matter. (So, move over, Grandma. That eighty-inch TV on sale is *mine!*) This, actually, is normal. Since we live our lives twenty-four/seven through our own eyes, of course we are going to naturally want everything to work out for us first and foremost. It may take a little bit of time to relax, calm down, and see the other person's point of view.

So when I realized my mistake and my embarrassment set in, from my own egocentric perspective, I thought I was the main character in everyone's life and they were still thinking about it. And for those long twenty minutes, no one would have been able to tell me otherwise. However, I soon realized that my life was not any different than it would have been if I had sung those lyrics correctly. The narrative I was telling myself simply was not true. Nobody cared then, and nobody cares now what I was singing. Seriously, nobody friggin' cares. I can confidently say that nobody is thinking of that today. However, for those twenty minutes, I thought my mishap was at the forefront of everyone's mind when, in reality, we know that just is not true. I am not the star in their show. They are. We all have our own shows that we are the stars in. We have a few costars, of course, but everyone else can be considered a walk-on. I learned I was just a walk-on in their shows. And I was totally okay with that.

I realized I had fallen victim to living in the feeling of what I *thought* and not in the feeling of what was *real*.

I know you know what I mean. How many times have you done that?

Have you ever noticed when something funny or embarrassing happens to someone else, you think it's funny? I am referring to silly, nonthreatening things, of course, such as getting lyrics wrong. This reminds me of the time I was nine months pregnant, sitting with my sister down the shore on the beach. We had our chairs down by the water, enjoying the refreshing ocean waves that were keeping our feet cool. A wave came in strong and ended up getting our towels and beach bags wet. As the waves started to go back out toward the ocean, I laughed out loud and said, "Ha ha, there goes your phone!" I was hysterically laughing, thinking she had to go chase her phone into the ocean. Then she looked at me and said, "That's not my phone. My phone is here in my hand." All of a sudden, it was no longer funny to me as I now realized it was *my* phone being washed away! As I tried to get my very pregnant self out of my chair, my sister was now the one laughing. I retrieved my phone after almost toppling over. And yes, a trip to the phone store was in my immediate future. To this day, she tells the story and laughs.

What did I learn? I learned that before I overreact to situations that happen to me, I think of what I would say if someone told me the same story happening to them. If I would laugh, then I know it does not deserve my energy to worry.

Here's what I want you to get from this chapter: pick and choose your battles as well as your worries. Sure, you may biologically need to be right. But now that you're aware of this need, you can work on not placing so much emphasis on winning every battle. Think of what the endgame is. If we constantly gratified our need to be right, we would be downright unbearable. I certainly have bigger things to think about than whether I got the lyrics wrong for twenty years. So give yourself some grace. No matter what the situation is, remember that nobody is perfect.

If you do this, in the exact moment when you are mortified or feel like something is the end of the world, you will learn to replace that with humor and lightheartedness. You'll realize that nobody is paying attention to these little things. And if they do, they won't remember. They are busy worrying about the same things in their own lives.

When you master that belief, that is where freedom begins!

Chapter 3

The Power of Laughter

*"You don't stop laughing because you grow older, you
grow older because you stop laughing."*

—Maurice Chevalier

Daddio was a huge proponent of laughter. He could find
humor in anything. While he was sensitive to delicate
situations, he believed a certain degree of laughter could help
anyone escape even the most difficult times, even if just for a
moment.

When I came back home to start my life over, I moved back
into my parents' house. They had a treadmill, a.k.a. clothes
hanger, and I decided to clear my mind and start using it.
One particular day, I required a long run to get my thoughts

in order. I figured if I could get my thoughts in order, then maybe my life wasn't such a mess. I started running on the treadmill, and I soon worked up an incredible sweat. I had a water bottle, the kind with a spout, sitting on the kitchen counter. When I got off the treadmill, I went into the kitchen to retrieve it and took a much-needed gulp to quench my thirst. Immediately, I had to spit out what was in my mouth. What I didn't know was that my dad had taken off the top and placed a piece of tissue in the spout. So when I started drinking, all I got was gooey, wet tissue in my mouth. As I realized something gross was happening, I looked up and saw him laughing hysterically in the corner. All I could do was laugh with him. A much-needed laugh at that!

So, I ask you. Who doesn't love laughter? Who doesn't love humor? Who doesn't love the feeling they get when they are laughing their butt off with friends?

I have never met anybody who would rather be grumpy than laugh. I'm not saying I haven't met grumpy people. I'm saying that if grumpy people allowed themselves to laugh, they would have a happier life. That's a fact.

Laughter is fun, but did you know that it actually also has health benefits? It does! And guess what. You don't have to go for a jog or eat something that tastes like cardboard to do something good for yourself and your body! Instead, you can *laugh*. Laughter has both short-term and long-term benefits. Without getting all technical and boring about how the human body works, I'll explain.

In the short term, laughter can stimulate many organs. It enhances your intake of oxygen; stimulates your heart, lungs, and muscles; and increases the endorphins that your brain releases. Laughter can also aid in circulation and muscle relaxation, both of which can help reduce some of the physical symptoms of stress.

Long-term effects can improve your mind. Studies have shown that laughter can help lessen stress, depression, and anxiety, and it may make you feel happier. Neurotransmitters, like dopamine, are also released, contributing to the pleasure response.

Physiologically, laughter promotes relaxation and boosts the immune system. Socially, it strengthens bonds, enhances communication, and creates connections. Laughter often involves social interaction, providing a sense of support and further helping us temporarily forget our worries. Have you ever gone out with some friends, had a fantastic time with lots of laughs, and at the very end of the night, turned to your friends and said, "Thanks! I needed that"?

Of course you have! That's the power of laughter.

Simply stated, laughter has a therapeutic effect on your mental state. It can momentarily shift your focus away from troubles, reduce stress, and create a positive mindset. Learning to laugh at things involves adopting a more lighthearted perspective. It's about embracing humor, finding the absurdity in situations, and not taking everything too seriously. Developing a sense of humor allows for resilience, helping you navigate challenges with a positive outlook. It's a skill that promotes mental flexibility, coping mechanisms, and a more enjoyable approach to life's ups and downs.

Now, I'm not saying to just laugh everything off. Every situation carries both positive and negative aspects. It's a matter of perspective and interpretation. Recognizing the positive side can lead to growth, learning, and resilience while acknowledging that the negative side allows for realistic assessment and preparation. Learning how to navigate these two aspects helps you maintain a balanced mindset while encouraging adaptability throughout each individual circumstance.

Yeah, but my situation isn't a laughing matter, you might be thinking. And that may be true. Trust me, I have had far more serious situations happen to me besides the ones I have shared with you so far. Finding humor in challenging situations doesn't mean dismissing the seriousness of your circumstances. Instead, it involves acknowledging the difficulties while opting to see the lighter side. It means taking a step back, knowing that you will get through this. Humor can be a coping mechanism, providing a mental break and helping you plot a route through tough times with a more resilient mindset. It's about finding a balance between recognizing the gravity of a situation and allowing yourself moments of relief through laughter.

Besides, you'll save on Botox. That shit is expensive. It takes more muscles to frown (around forty-three) than to smile (only about seventeen). Additionally, repetitive facial expressions, like frowning, can contribute to the development of wrinkles over time due to muscles contracting and skin folding. Smiling, on the other hand, may have a more positive impact on facial appearance.

What better reason to laugh?

You may want to share that information with what's her name, a.k.a. "resting bitch face." You know who I mean . . . We ALL know one of them.

It is important to note that humor is a powerful tool for improving your mindset and overall well-being. Here's how it can positively impact your mental state:

1. It can reduce stress.

As stated above, laughter triggers the release of endorphins, which are the body's natural feel-good chemicals. This helps reduce stress and promote a sense of relaxation, even in challenging situations.

(Now, I am confident that you can think of other things that can reduce stress besides laughter. However, laughter is neither immoral, illegal, nor fattening like those other things probably are, so stick with humor. Trust me on this one.)

2. It can enhance your mood.

Humor can instantly lift your spirits, shifting your mindset from negative to positive. It provides a momentary escape from worries and can improve your overall emotional state. And no hangover!

3. It can improve your resilience.

A sense of humor can strengthen your ability to cope with adversity. It allows you to see difficulties from a different perspective and find lightness even in challenging moments.

4. It enhances your social connections.

Sharing laughter with others strengthens social bonds. Positive interactions and shared humor can lead to better relationships, reducing feelings of isolation and loneliness. For example, going to a comedy show. Even if you were to go by yourself, there is a feeling of camaraderie when laughing together even if you do not know the other people. Same for funny movies. It's much more fun to watch with someone else who is sharing the laughter!

5. It encourages creative problem-solving.

Humor can help you approach issues from different angles, leading to more effective solutions. Your brain absorbs more and thinks more clearly when you are in a good mood.

6. It helps you stop procrastinating.

If you are a procrastinator, think about trying to meet a deadline that you probably are nowhere close to meeting. Thoughts are probably swirling around in your head, and you are waiting for one of them to land, almost like you do not know where to begin. Laughter can help replace the stress and get the ideas flowing. How do I know? I am a recovering procrastinator.

7. It increases productivity.

A lighthearted atmosphere in the workplace can boost productivity. People who can find humor in their tasks tend to be more motivated and efficient. Think about it. When you are in a less-than-good mood and do not get yourself to a better mindset, the day seems to become a spiral effect of mishaps. Using humor and positivity at the onset of a challenge will help you not only get through that individual task but also help you navigate your day in a different, more pleasant direction.

8. It forges a mind-body connection.

As previously stated, laughter and humor can have physical benefits, such as reducing muscle tension, improving blood flow, and boosting the immune system, all of which contribute to an overall positive mindset.

9. It promotes self-reflection.

Humor can help you take yourself less seriously. It allows for self-reflection without self-criticism, helping you maintain a more balanced and forgiving self-image, in turn reducing negative self-talk. In other words, learn to laugh at yourself. I laugh every time I tell the story of the day I "lost" my sunglasses. I went running back into the store I'd just spent an hour shopping in and frantically searched the entire place. Nothing. Someone took them. But I'd just been there! These thieves are so fast. So I marched up to the courtesy desk and annoyingly asked if anyone had turned in a pair of sunglasses because, as I curtly said to the elderly lady listening to me, "I cannot believe people in this store would take them." That's when the elderly lady behind the counter sweetly looked at me and calmly said, "Do you mean the sunglasses on top of your head?" I quickly made a silly joke and left. Thank goodness for humor.

10. It promotes a positive perspective.

Humor often involves looking at situations with more positive eyes. It encourages you to find joy in the ordinary and appreciate life's small pleasures, resulting in an attitude of gratitude.

11. It promotes stress resilience.

Developing a sense of humor can build resilience in dealing with life's ups and downs. It equips you with a valuable tool to navigate challenges with a lighter heart. It allows you to recognize and acknowledge that a situation has become difficult and helps you choose a reaction that leads to growth. It's so much more effective than immediately freaking out.

So again, I am not saying you should go through life laughing at everything. Of course, life will hand you some serious situations that are not laughable. What I am saying is if you learn to laugh at the everyday mishaps and learn to look at the brighter side of everyday situations, when major occurrences do take place, you will be better equipped to handle them. Whether it is the death of a family member, a bad health diagnosis, or the loss of a job, for example, you will be able to persevere through it because you have trained your mindset to go back to its default setting, which is happiness and positivity.

It's important to note that humor is highly individual, and what one person finds funny, another might not. Trust me, there have been plenty of times when I thought I was being hilarious, and it turned out to be a party of one. The key is to find what makes you laugh and incorporate it into your life regularly. Whether through comedy, jokes, funny movies, or simply finding joy in everyday moments, embracing humor can be a powerful strategy for maintaining a positive mindset and improving your overall mental health.

Besides, life is not only easier with a sense of humor. It is a hell of a lot more fun.

Chapter 4

Manage Your Mindset

"Positive thinking will let you do everything better than negative thinking will."

—Zig Ziglar

Mindset, mindset, mindset.

"Change your mindset, change your life."

"A positive mindset brings positive things."

"Mindset is everything."

Blah, blah, blah. You have heard them all. But guess what? They are all true. However, unless you understand what mindset is, how can you change it? What exactly is mindset?

And, more importantly, do you control it? Or does it control you?

Mindset refers to the established set of attitudes, beliefs, and perceptions that shape how you approach and interpret the world around you. It influences how you handle situations, how you make decisions, and how you respond to challenges.

Living with a dad who was a motivational speaker, it was difficult to maintain a negative mindset for very long. As we were growing up and going through each stage of the teenage years, we certainly had our share of what we thought were "problems." But Daddio was like the bumpers at a bowling alley, keeping us in the positive lane and not letting us falter into the negative alley. We still managed to go there at times, but having his positive vibe sure did help us not stay there.

Positive or negative influences in your surroundings can play a significant role in shaping your attitudes and outlook on life. Here are a few of the key elements that can affect your mindset.

1. Nutrition

What you eat can have a significant impact on your mood and cognitive function. So, put down the daily double cheeseburger and fries. Being mindful of your dietary choices can contribute to a more stable and positive mindset. For example, if you eat a lot of refined sugar (candy, cakes, cookies, etc.), you will get what is known as a "sugar rush," where dopamine is released at lightning speed. Unfortunately, as fast as the dopamine high comes in, it retreats even faster, leaving you feeling sluggish, disinterested, and even stressed. Therefore, you will be handling situations with a stressed mindset, as if everything is annoying or a problem. Yes! Lack of good nutrition can do that to you! Now, I'm not saying you should become a vegan tomorrow. (I did that once, and it was the worst two hours of my life! Kudos to all you vegans.) But I am saying you should start incorporating healthier snacks, such as fruit. Soon, you can start to replace a meal with a healthy balance of protein, vegetables, and complex carbohydrates. Then replace two meals with the same. Soon, you will gravitate toward healthy choices for every meal and only occasionally partake in the not-so-healthy foods. When you do this, you will feel better and, therefore, be more positive. Try it!

2. Social environment

The people you surround yourself with play a key role in shaping your mindset. I can hear my mom saying now, "You are judged by the company you keep. Soon, you will be acting and thinking just like them!" And she, as always, was right!

That goes both ways. Positive relationships can provide support, encouragement, and connection. Conversely, negative influences can contribute to stress and negativity. Being aware of toxic relationships and prioritizing positive connections can greatly influence your overall mindset. Stop complaining just because that's how your best friend acts. She's frigging annoying. (More on this later.)

3. Media consumption

The content you consume, whether through news, social media, or entertainment, can shape your perceptions and mindset. Being conscious of the media you expose yourself to allows you to filter out negativity and choose content that aligns with your values and promotes a positive mindset. And let's face it. Much of the social media you see today is nothing but negative. Pick and choose wisely. Even reading and/or watching something will affect you. Don't get caught in the scroll hole, being a zombie and subconsciously absorbing all that crap.

4. Personal habits

Daily habits, such as exercise, sleep, and mindfulness practices, also impact your mindset. Regular physical activity, sufficient sleep, and mindfulness techniques contribute to overall well-being and a more positive mental state. Consistency is key here. I'm not saying you have to work out at the gym every day like you are entering a competition, but daily exercise, such as walking, yoga, and weight training, as well as mindfulness practices (yoga, meditation, breath work) will help you get a better night's sleep. These habits, in turn, will impact your mindset positively.

Change Your Environment, Change Your Life

Here's the thing: If you want to change your mindset, start by changing your environment. Of all the factors I listed above, perhaps the two most crucial, in my opinion, are the company you surround yourself with and the food you eat. In fact, being mindful of these is crucial for maintaining a positive and healthy mental outlook. First, let's talk more about the people you spend time with.

I had a mentor who once said, "Show me who you spend the most time with, and I will show you who you *are* or who you *will be*." Yikes! But it is true. This goes along with the adage, "You are the sum of the five people you spend the most time with," and it really made a lot of sense. You actually become a product of your environment. If you are consistently around negative people, you have no choice but to see things in a negative way. The good news is it's the same if you are around positive people. You will start to see things in a positive way.

Avoid negative people at all costs, for they are the greatest destroyers of self-confidence and self-esteem. Surround yourself with people who bring out the best in you.

Now look, I know there are some people you just cannot boot out of your life. That negative, annoying family member or that coworker who gossips, for example. But you can *limit* your association. You are probably thinking, *Hey, I can't always get away from family or the people who affect my mindset in a negative way. How do I avoid that?* Well, my top suggestion would be to run away from it all and start a new life in Costa Rica. But since most people cannot do that, here are some suggestions.

1. Set boundaries.

Clearly communicate your boundaries and expectations. Let others know what behavior is unacceptable, and establish limits to protect your well-being. Honor your boundaries. You can't be everything to everyone and nothing to yourself. That's counterintuitive to why you are here. Limit the conversations you have with negative people and the energy you exchange. Tell Sally at the water fountain that you do not care who the new girl is sleeping with. (Unless, of course, it is your husband. Then stick around and get some more details.) Remember, you don't need to be invested or involved in everything that goes on around you, no matter who it is—family, friends, or coworkers. Recognize that drama is an unconscious behavior for some people. It is how they live their lives. It may be a learned behavior from their environment or their search for validation. Protect your energy from all of it.

2. Choose your battles.

Not every disagreement requires confrontation. Pick your battles wisely, and focus on addressing issues that have a significant impact on your mindset and overall happiness. Walk away. You do not always have to live your life like an episode of *Judge Judy*. Trust me, walking away is better than trying to make someone see that you are right. (Unless, of course, you are a trial lawyer. Then, well, you kind of have to battle on, or you're going to have one mad client. If that is the case, I hope they look good in orange.)

3. Seek support.

Surround yourself with positive influences, and seek support from friends or other family members who understand your perspective. Having a support system can provide emotional reinforcement. This doesn't mean forming teams against each other. That is just a recipe for a very uncomfortable holiday dinner. But it does mean placing more of your energy with the people who live in the drama-free zone.

4. Practice self-care.

Invest time in activities that promote your mental and emotional well-being. Whether it's engaging in hobbies, exercise, meditation, walks in nature, or positive affirmations, prioritizing self-care will build resilience against negative influences. Soon, you will recognize negativity immediately, and your mind and body will respond accordingly. It will repel any negative energy, and you will innately know that you do not want to be a part of it.

5. Communicate.

Express your feelings calmly and assertively. Effective communication can help others understand your perspective and contribute to a healthier relationship dynamic. Believe it or not, positivity is like mosquito repellant to negativity and negative people. After a time, negative people won't even approach you. It's like a protective barrier.

6. Get professional help.

If necessary, consider seeking the assistance of a therapist or counselor (or mindset mentor!) to help you heal family dynamics and develop coping strategies. Some people do not even realize they are having a negative effect on others. Professional guidance can be valuable in challenging situations. It can be helpful to seek a neutral party since most people see things from their own point of view. (There's that egocentric thing again.)

Remember, as I stated earlier, avoiding negativity doesn't necessarily mean cutting ties completely. It's about creating a healthy balance and finding ways to protect your mindset while maintaining relationships that are important to you. Especially that relationship with yourself.

You Are What You Think

So, how does your mindset differ from how you think?

I'm glad you asked.

Mindset and thinking are closely related concepts, but they differ in their scope and nature.

Mindset is a broader term that encompasses your entire mental framework. Remember, it involves attitudes, beliefs, and perceptions that influence overall behavior and decision-making. Mindset is like the lens through which you view the world and approach various aspects of life. For example, either believing you are going to have a great day or, conversely, believing you are going to have a bad day is a mindset.

Thinking is a more specific and immediate cognitive process. It refers to the mental activities and processes involved in forming thoughts, making decisions, and solving problems. Thinking can be influenced by your mindset, but it also includes moment-to-moment cognitive activities. As in the mindset example, thinking would be breaking down your day into all the things you can be grateful for or, conversely, everything that could go wrong.

In essence, mindset is the big picture, while thinking is the specific cognitive activity that occurs within that mindset. A positive mindset can influence positive thinking, leading to effective positive thought patterns and decisions.

Have you ever heard the phrase "Your mind is the strongest muscle in your body"? This is a metaphor emphasizing the incredible power and influence of the mind. While the mind is not a literal muscle, the comparison highlights its ability to shape thoughts, emotions, and actions. While physical muscles are essential for bodily functions, the metaphor shows the immense influence of the mind in shaping your responses, behaviors, and overall quality of life. But be careful because the mind is so strong that you can literally think your way into justifying any action the body takes, even the negative ones.

For example, the employee who steals from their employer will justify it by saying, "Oh well, they don't pay me enough, and I do so much overtime that I don't get paid for. So I took a little extra money." Or the wife who cheats on her husband will justify it by saying, "Oh well, he's a workaholic and never home anyway. He never listens to my thoughts or problems. I needed someone."

The problem here is that using "my mind said it was okay" will never hold up as a defense in court!

Having a positive mindset is crucial in helping your decision-making. Without stress impacting your judgment, you can make clearer, better decisions. A positive mindset has a tumbleweed effect. In other words, once you get rolling into the habit of thinking positively, you train your mind to see the good. Positivity is a choice. You decide if you want to be positive. Your happiness depends on the quality of your thoughts, so it only makes sense to keep high-quality, positive thoughts. Positivity can affect your:

1. Perception and interpretation
2. Willpower and motivation
3. Emotional regulation
4. Adaptability
5. Self-belief
6. Problem-solving

Perception and Interpretation

The mind interprets and gives meaning to experiences. It determines how you perceive challenges, setbacks, and successes, shaping your overall outlook on life. Rather than being quick to react and automatically thinking a situation is awful, it helps to bring the brighter side to the surface.

Willpower and Motivation

Mental strength plays a crucial role in willpower and motivation. A positive mindset can give you the drive to overcome obstacles, pursue goals, and stay focused on long-term objectives. Mindset over matter.

Emotional Regulation

The mind influences emotional responses and how well you manage stress. A strong mind can help regulate emotions, leading to greater resilience and overall well-being. (See Anxiety/Stress in the next chapter.)

Adaptability

The mind's flexibility and adaptability are vital. It helps you navigate change, learn from experiences, and adjust to different situations.

Self-Belief

Confidence and self-belief stem from the mind. A positive mindset can boost self-esteem, enabling you to face challenges with a sense of capability and assurance.

Problem-Solving

A strong mindset allows you to approach challenges with creativity and find effective solutions. This actually becomes a by-product of self-belief. A positive mindset gives you confidence, which gives you the belief in yourself you need to approach various situations competently.

Encouraging a growth mindset, in which you focus on possibilities and opportunities, brings about perseverance, adaptability, and an overall more positive outlook. Instead of arguing for limitations, you want to strive to challenge and overcome them, embracing the potential for personal and professional growth.

I realize that it is not always easy these days, in a time when the world is changing, money is tight, and values differ. The world's mode of operation is to grab that one negative thing that is happening among all the positive things. Negativity does not require growth or work, which is why it is so easy to gravitate toward it. There is a valid reason why there is an entire industry built on personal development. Remember, people want instant gratification. They want validation. It is easier to get both of those things by running with the negative and not having to strive for the positive. Why? While positivity has greater rewards, nine times out of ten, the situation mandates that you go through something a bit more strenuous on either the mind or the body to get to that positive result.

People will sometimes tell me, "Well, I woke up positive yesterday, and nothing good happened."

A positive mindset doesn't just happen, like turning on a light switch. You have to be committed to it daily. And that commitment requires personal growth. It was the late, great Zig Ziglar who compared nurturing personal growth and a positive mindset to taking a bath. To paraphrase, he explained that you must do personal growth every single day, just as you would take a bath. Otherwise, you stink. Your attitude stinks. Your mindset stinks. The way you handle things stinks. It is a daily behavior. Consistency is key. Remember, Rome wasn't built in a day. The Romans didn't put a couple of bricks up and say, "Oh yeah. You know what? This isn't happening fast enough. Let's just forget about Rome. Who needs an empire anyway?" No, they kept at it.

I will say it again. It is all about consistency. Discipline and consistency. You can do it. Think back to when you were little. You had to be told every single day to brush your teeth. Otherwise, you forgot. Before you knew it, you didn't have to be told to brush your teeth. You were consistent, and it became a habit.

Personal growth is the same way. Once you do some form of personal growth every single day—whether it be reading ten pages out of a book, meditating, praying, practicing positive affirmations, whatever—then you will get up and do it just like you brush your teeth. (Unless you have really bad oral hygiene. Then, in that case, it's a terrible example.)

I can't say it enough. When it comes to mindset, what is key? Right! Consistency! Think of a time when you felt like you had completely lost control of your day. Well, having that thought alone was a self-fulfilling prophecy. You already said you couldn't get ahold of your day, so guess what? You didn't have control of your day!

That's another example of where consistency comes in. Instead of immediately saying you don't have control of your day, commit to a morning and an evening routine. If you have control of your morning routine and you have control of your evening routine, with consistency, the rest will fall into place. Even if you start out just having a morning routine, that's okay! Soon, a night routine will be added.

This reminds me of Admiral William H. McRaven's commencement address at the University of Texas at Austin in 2014. Admiral McRaven, a retired Navy SEAL, highlighted the significance of the small task of making your bed as a way to start the day with discipline and accomplishment. His speech, titled "Make Your Bed" (go figure, right?), emphasized the importance of simple actions and their potential impact on one's mindset and success.

I totally agree! So much so that if my son left the house without making his bed, I would call him wherever he was and remind him that he didn't make his bed. He got so sick of me calling him when he was with his friends that he made his bed every time he left the house. (Yes, I was *that* mom.) And when he was a young boy, his bed-making certainly couldn't make a quarter bounce. But he was doing it and starting his day with consistency and discipline.

So, if you have a morning routine you can stick to and an evening routine you can stick to, you are in control of your morning and your evening. That pattern of behavior will soon spread throughout your day, and the gap will get smaller and smaller and smaller. Before you know it, you will have control over your whole day.

Now, that's not to say unexpected situations won't arise during your day. It just means that over time, these situations will be easier to handle as you become more intentional and more in control of your day.

As I was writing this book, I had some pretty chaotic days with some pretty chaotic thoughts going on in my head.

Imagine! A mindset mentor with a poor mindset! Yes, I am human. So I, too, had a lapse of letting a poor mindset take over. I started to doubt myself, stress out a bit, and even wonder if I was going to be able to help anyone with this book. But I knew I had a lot of information to share, and I knew it had to get out there to reach whomever it needed to reach. I focused on that instead of the doubt, and my actions soon followed my thoughts.

We *all* go through those less-than-stellar times. When that happens, remember this: Negativity is contagious. Unhappiness is contagious. Fear is contagious. But so is happiness. So is optimism. So is love.

Train your mind to see the good in everything. Because life is like a battery. Where there is a negative, there is a positive. Positivity is a choice. Your happiness depends on the quality of your thoughts. Surround yourself with people who bring out the best in you, and strive to be a reflection of what you want to receive. *You* control your mindset.

Remember, your mindset starts with an intention. Then a behavior. Then a habit. Then a practice. Then second nature. Then it is simply who you are.

Chapter 5

Anxiety and the (Anti) Social Media

"No one can make you feel inferior without your consent."

—Eleanor Roosevelt

I love that quote. In fact, it is my favorite. Think about it—it is so true! Why do we allow the words of others to become our truth? I especially love the quote because Eleanor Roosevelt said it. Allow me to explain.

Eleanor Roosevelt was the wife of President Franklin D. Roosevelt and served as the First Lady of the United States from 1933 to 1945. It was during this time, the 1930s, that pinup beauties, such as Bette Davis, Lana Turner, Veronica Lake, and Vivian Leigh, graced the silver screen. This era soon became known as the Golden Age of Glamour. Those starlets set the precedent for what was to be desirable and beautiful. The bar was set high, and most every woman tried to achieve this beauty standard. However, the First Lady was not on the big screen and was, how do I put this . . . well, NOT glamorous. However, she knew who she was: a United Nations diplomat, an activist, a humanitarian, and, in her time, one of the world's most admired and powerful women. Imagine if she had allowed society or others to determine her worth.

In this chapter, we'll explore the effects of negative self-talk, anxiety, and social media together. (However, as you can see, I referred to social media as the anti-social media because that is exactly what it is making our society.)

I feel as though anxiety and negative self-talk can both easily be by-products of social media, so let's talk about that first.

The Anti-Social Media

Ah, social media. First, I will say there are some benefits to it. It enables people all around the world to stay in touch. Posting pictures allows friends and family to see your kids growing up, your last adventure, or even what you ate for dinner, should they so choose. (Quite frankly, I never understood that one.

But hey, bon appétit!) It allows people to promote worthwhile causes for the good of humanity. It can help you market your business or product. And, of course, it allows you to see how fat or bald your ex has gotten. *Bonus.*

However, I can honestly say that social media has astoundingly changed our society, and, in many ways, not for the better. It has taken over adults' and kids' lives alike and has affected the human race in damaging ways.

Now, I realize we must move forward with changing times, but when the changing times become detrimental to society, precautions must be taken. Here are some ways social media can affect your mindset:

1. It can leave you feeling that you are inadequate.

You know that the images you are viewing on social media are manipulated, so why are you allowing them to make you feel that way? Photo filters. They are right up there with the best inventions, such as caller ID, GPS, and my personal favorite, the epidural for labor pain. (I do not know for sure, but I would bet they were all invented by women! Because let's face it, a man would never ask for directions even from a GPS.) Anyway, back to photo filters . . . They can make even the creature from the Black Lagoon look like a mermaid. Everyone knows this. However, those Photoshopped, filtered pictures can still make you feel insecure about how you look or how you feel about what is going on in your own life. Not to mention that people tend to share just the highlights of their lives and *rarely* the low points that everyone experiences. That's a fact that is always overlooked. Their goal is to make it look like their lives are perfect and easy. For instance, if I see one more "Boss Babe" sitting on her kitchen counter with her laptop to press the point that you can do her business from anywhere, I just might lose my cookies. *Anywhere?* And you chose your kitchen counter? Come on, girl.

2. It can give you fear of missing out.

FOMO has been around far longer than social media sites. However, these platforms seem to falsely portray other people having more fun than you and, therefore, having a better life than you. The idea that you are missing out on certain things can impact your self-esteem and/or trigger anxiety. This is where that comparison factor can be seen. Constantly checking your social media to see if you and your life stand up to others can turn social media into an addiction of sorts. The fear of missing out can pressure you to pick up your phone every few minutes to check for updates or likes on your own or others' posts. This can make social media interactions seem more important than real-life relationships.

3. It can cause depression and anxiety.

Plain and simple, human beings need face-to-face contact to be mentally healthy. Hugging, conversation, energy exchanges, and even just eye-to-eye contact all contribute to reducing stress and boosting your mood, especially with a loved one or someone who cares about you. Or even just a nice person you encounter in your travels! The more you prioritize social media interaction over in-person relationships, the more likely mood disorders, such as anxiety or depression, can develop. *And* the more likely you could "fall in love" online with the sixty-five-year-old bald man whose profile pic makes you believe he's a dead ringer for Brad Pitt.

4. It can cause you to be self-absorbed.

If anything is going to distance you from real-life connections, it's the guy or girl who insists on posting *everything* about themselves on social media. Yes, that one. The never-ending selfie queen or king. (Hey, queen, it's your page. Do what you want. But seriously, I think by now, we all have an idea of what your boobs look like. But go ahead and chalk up those likes. That's important. I guess.)

5. It hosts cyberbullying.

This is one of the worst things about social media, in my opinion. About 10 percent of teens report being bullied on social media, and many other users are subjected to offensive comments. Social media platforms are a breeding ground for hurtful rumors and lies, as well as abuse that can leave lasting emotional scars, and sometimes worse. The number of keyboard warriors who use social media as a means to elevate their own false self-esteem by degrading or bullying others is astounding. Funny thing is, get face-to-face with these same people, and they are often nothing like the torturers they are behind the screen.

These are just some of the by-products of social media and why I have dubbed it anti-social media. Trying to keep up with the highly inflated personas exhibited on social media can lead to many of the mood disorders found today, as well as a breakdown of relationships due to noncommunication. While not solely responsible for the following topics, social media can be contributing to the rise of negative self-talk and anxiety.

Negative Self-Talk

Negative self-talk can have profound and detrimental effects on your well-being and overall mental health. It acts as a relentless internal critic, chipping away at self-esteem and confidence. The average person thinks as many as fifty thousand thoughts a day. Unfortunately, around 85 percent of them are negative.

"I'm fat."

"Of course this didn't work out. Nothing ever works out for me."

"He would never want to go out with me."

This is victim language, and it will actually keep you in a victim mentality, eventually training your mind to believe that you are unworthy and/or unlovable.

Studies have shown that negative self-talk is most prominent in women. Insecurities and low self-esteem are common among the female population. But why? Little girls younger than five certainly aren't that way. They dance and sing, jump and play, and even pretend (and believe!) that they are princesses. So what happens?

Unfortunately, a lot of women had their first experience with insecurities at the hands of other women. Their mother or aunts could have made them feel insecure or inferior by scrutinizing their appearance. Comparing themselves to sisters or friends may have started an inferiority complex, which could give some women a sense of worthlessness, making them feel as though they are constantly in a competition.

Society's false depictions of women can also be detrimental to a woman's sense of self. Many women feel they have an unconscious obligation to compete with others, especially other women. I would tell them this: Your competition isn't other people. Your competition is your procrastination. Your ego. Your own self-sabotaging thoughts. So just stop! Because if you don't make a conscious effort to shut off the negative self-talk in your head, it becomes a huge tumbleweed of doom and gloom.

Here are some of the ways negative self-talk can impact you:

1. It can cause low self-esteem.

Negative self-talk reinforces feelings of inadequacy and worthlessness. Over time, you may come to believe you are incapable of achieving or are undeserving of success and happiness.

2. It can lead to anxiety and depression.

Constant self-criticism can contribute to the development of anxiety and depression. It creates a cycle in which negative thoughts fuel negative emotions, leading to a downward spiral of mental health.

3. It can stifle your potential.

Negative self-talk can lead you to underestimate your abilities and avoid taking risks. This can hinder personal and professional growth, preventing you from reaching your full potential.

4. It can impair your relationships.

If you engage in negative self-talk, you may struggle with interpersonal relationships. You may project your self-doubt onto others, leading to conflicts and strained connections. This is when negative self-talk and low self-esteem can lead to distrust of a partner even though they show no signs of disloyalty.

5. It can impact your physical health.

The stress and anxiety generated by negative self-talk can take a toll on physical health. It has been linked to an increased heart rate, higher blood pressure, and a weakened immune system.

6. It can lead to perfectionism.

Negative self-talk often drives perfectionism. You may set unrealistically high standards for yourself, leading to chronic stress and dissatisfaction. No one thinks they are a perfectionist, but when push comes to shove, no one wants to be the one who is wrong. Perfection is the illusion that often holds us back. Remember, nobody is flawless, and that is what makes us beautifully unique. Learn to embrace imperfections as opportunities for growth and learning. Strive for progress, not perfection, as you will always reach the progress mark but never the perfection mark.

7. It can create self-fulfilling prophecies.

When you constantly tell yourself that you will fail, you are more likely to fulfill that prophecy. Negative self-talk can become a self-fulfilling cycle of failure and disappointment. A self-fulfilling prophecy is a belief or expectation that influences behavior in such a way that it causes the belief to come true. In other words, anticipating a certain outcome can lead to actions and behaviors that make that outcome more likely. Your brain looks for evidence to support it, and, therefore, the belief naturally becomes your mode of operation.

For example, if someone believes they will fail at a task, this belief might affect their attitude and effort, ultimately contributing to a negative result. On the other hand, having a positive expectation can lead to behaviors that increase the likelihood of a positive outcome.

8. It can cause you to ruminate.

Negative self-talk can lead to rumination, which means constantly dwelling on your mistakes or perceived shortcomings, making it difficult to focus on the present and find solutions to problems. You know that person who always talks about how they are not "good in relationships" because they are divorced or do not have a significant other? They are continually focused on what didn't work out, so they are not open to finding out why it didn't work out or how they can be happy right now.

9. It can reduce your resilience.

Those who engage in negative self-talk are less likely to be resilient when facing challenges. They may give up easily or view setbacks as a sign of perceived outcomes. They automatically think the end result is going to be awful, so why even bother? Continuing with the relationship example, rather than reframing the situation in a positive light, setting realistic goals, and celebrating any progress, they give up on the relationship quickly with the notion that "this isn't going to work."

10. It can lead to social isolation.

Over time, the impact of negative self-talk can lead to social withdrawal. You may isolate yourself, believing that others are better off without you. You have the mentality that if you don't like you, then how will others like you?

You may have experienced some of these effects, and if you are being honest with yourself, you know that you have. Sometimes we engage in negative self-talk without even realizing it. For example, let's say you see a woman with beautiful, long hair. The first thought that pops into your head is, *Wow, what beautiful hair*. That's fine. That is only an observation. However, when you follow it up with *I wish my hair was that pretty*, that's when the negative self-talk enters. The comparison starts, and the feelings of inadequacy begin.

We do this a lot. *Stop it*. Become okay with observing someone or something without the automatic competition in your mind.

Let's say I asked you, "What is the longest relationship you have ever had"? What would your answer be? A romantic partner? A best friend? A sibling? Your parents?

Nope, all wrong.

It's *you! You* are the longest relationship you have ever had or ever will have. It has been you since you were in utero. You are with *you* twenty-four hours a day, seven days a week. *You* know yourself better than anyone knows you. You can never escape *you*. You will never speak to anyone more than you speak to yourself in your head.

I often do an exercise with people to bring their negative self-talk to the forefront, whether it be in their everyday life or in business. One particular instance was with a woman who was trying to push her business further. I told her to give me three things about herself that she believed might be holding her back. She said, "I'm not good at sales, people don't seem to respond to me, and I don't think I am pretty enough." We then did a role-play in which I acted as a friend calling her for lunch. Here's the CliffsNotes version of how it went:

"Hey, Joan. It's Beth. Want to go check out that new sushi place today?"

"Oh, I can't. I have to meet a potential client."

"Potential client? For what?"

"For the business that I got into."

"What? You're still doing that thing? Listen, Joan. I gotta tell you, you are seriously wasting your time. I mean, you are really bad at sales. You couldn't sell water in the Sahara. I mean, you have to know that people just don't respond to you. And I can see why. I mean, you're certainly not winning any beauty contests, if you know what I mean. Go work at some nine-to-five job for the next forty years. At least you'll get a paycheck every week."

Okay, what?

Could you imagine hearing that from someone? Especially a so-called friend?

I don't know about you, but if anyone ever said that to me, I would have two words for them. And I guarantee you they would *not* be Happy Birthday!

But all I did was repeat back to her what she told me she told herself.

(And here's a side note: Don't ever let anyone call your business a "thing." The minute you accept someone referring to it as a "thing" is the minute that your subconscious accepts it as just a thing, too).

So I ask you, if you had to spend twenty-four/seven with another person, would you pick someone who did nothing but put you down or talk negatively to you and about you like that?

Of course not! Then stop doing it to yourself! *You* are that person you are spending twenty-four hours a day, seven days a week with! Every time you say something negative about yourself, imagine someone else saying it to you. It will hit you differently, and it will start to make you mindful of exactly how you talk to yourself. Be kind to yourself. Be mindful of your self-talk, for it is a conversation with the universe. Your mind will always believe everything you tell it. Feed it love. You will glow differently when your confidence is fueled by belief in yourself. There will always be someone who can't (or just won't!) see your worth. Don't let it be you.

Arguing for Your Limitations

Arguing for your limitations is another form of negative self-talk. That's when you reinforce negative beliefs about what you can't achieve or overcome. For example, a conversation might go something like this:

Friend #1: I can't focus enough to do that project. I have ADD.

Friend #2: Why don't you just do a little at a time each day?

Friend #1: Oh, that won't work. I have way too much going on around me at home. Lots of noise. Besides, I'll just start doing laundry or something.

Friend #2: Why don't you go to the library, where it's nice and quiet?

Friend #1: This week, I am so busy. I have too many things to do.

You get the picture. Friend #1 will continually argue for what she feels is her limitation—a lack of focus. A mindset like this can have several detrimental effects on personal growth and well-being:

1. It can lead to stagnation.

Accepting and arguing for limitations can lead to a lack of personal development. It creates a mental barrier that hinders progress, keeping you stuck in a comfort zone, which will absolutely hinder any growth or development. The only comfort zone you should be in is when you are relaxing and watching a movie with a big-ass bowl of popcorn. Other than that, stay out of the comfort zone.

2. It can cause missed opportunities.

Believing in limitations may cause you to overlook opportunities or shy away from challenges. It limits your ability to explore new possibilities and reach your full potential.

3. It can promote a negative mindset.

Continually arguing for limitations creates a negative mindset, affecting your overall outlook on life. It can lead to increased stress, lower self-esteem, and a diminished sense of accomplishment. Stop with the "Poor me" syndrome. It not only clouds your mindset, it lowers your chances of having a positive life experience.

4. It can lead to a self-fulfilling prophecy.

The more you argue for limitations, the more likely they are to become a self-fulfilling prophecy. Your beliefs can shape your actions, influencing the outcome to be in line with your negative expectations. The more you believe the limitations you have in your head, the sooner you will display the behavior that matches it.

5. It can have an impact on relationships.

A mindset focused on limitations can affect relationships. It may lead to feelings of inadequacy, hinder effective communication, and limit the ability to support others. Listen, it's pretty simple: nobody wants to be with a Debbie Downer. I get it. Sometimes sad things happen. However, when your mindset is consistently geared toward negativity, do not look around and wonder why you don't have a date to Cousin Mary's wedding. Food for thought: your good looks might get you into the party, but they won't keep you there. Stop being negative. Nobody wants to deal with that shit.

Addressing negative self-talk is extremely important for improving mental health and overall well-being. Health is not just about what you are eating or how you are physically feeling. It is also, and perhaps more importantly, about what you are thinking and saying.

You are worth so much more than how you make yourself feel when you talk negatively inside your head. If you do not know your own worth, people will give you what your perceived worth is. Show them how good you are by believing it yourself.

I promise you, when things change inside you, things will change around you.

Anxiety

anx·i·e·ty /aNGˈzīədē/

noun

a feeling of worry, nervousness, or unease, typically about an imminent event or something with an uncertain outcome.

"he felt a surge of anxiety"

Ah, yes. The dreaded anxiety. I'm sure you have felt the sensations of anxiety at least once in your life. Maybe it was before a job interview or perhaps when meeting a new beau's family for the first time. But why is anxiety worse for some people? Why do some people have challenges controlling their anxiety while others seem to skate through situations unscathed?

Well, if you ask me, I believe anxiety starts in the mind. And, as the definition states, it has you worrying about potential *future* events. The mindset associated with anxiety may involve excessive concern, fear of the unknown, or a sense of impending danger. This mental state triggers the body's stress response, known as the fight-or-flight response, even in situations that may not pose an immediate threat.

As the mind perceives a threat, or fear, it signals the release of stress hormones, like cortisol and adrenaline. These hormones prepare the body for action, thus leading to physical symptoms, such as increased heart rate, muscle tension, sweating, and panic attacks.

So what does that mean? In essence, it means anxiety starts in your mind and presents itself as a physical ailment. Once the physical ailment makes its appearance, the mind starts the worry and nervousness over that ailment. It is a spiral effect, and, at times, it's not easy to get yourself out of that spiral. Your original worry about the event that hasn't even happened is now overrun by your worry that something is happening to your body.

Now, that is not to say anxiety is not also genetic. Studies have shown that if you have anxiety, chances are another family member has anxiety. As a mindset mentor, however, I always start with learning how to control one's thoughts before the situation even gets to the body's response.

I had a friend say to me one time, "Oh, I have anxiety. It was inevitable. My mother has anxiety, my sister has anxiety, and even my grandmother has anxiety. Now my son has anxiety. We couldn't escape it!"

I gave her an answer she was *not* looking for. I explained that her reasoning reminded me of a person who once told me they were severely overweight because it "runs" in their family. They said, "Both my mom and dad are overweight. It's how we are shaped. It is hereditary."

Nope. It is not how you are shaped. It is because you and your mom and dad eat at the same table. Plain and simple.

They didn't like my answer either. Go figure.

So, I ask you, could it be that anxiety is the same situation? Maybe, just maybe, your mom saw how your grandmother handled situations, you saw how your mother handled situations, and your son sees how you handle situations. I'd be willing to bet that when he has children, they will see how *he* handles situations. And *surprise*! They just might end up with anxiety.

Addressing anxiety often involves not only managing the immediate physical symptoms but also addressing the thought patterns and mindset that were renting space in your head prior to the anxiety onset. Mindfulness practices, therapy, and other therapeutic approaches can help you break the cycle between the mind and the body, resulting in a more balanced and relaxed state.

This brings to mind the story of when I was in Atlantic City, New Jersey, eating in a restaurant. I went into the ladies' room and found a beautiful young woman on the floor. She was hunched over, fully conscious, eyes open, but her body was frozen in fear. After I asked her if she was alright, she confirmed that she was having a panic attack. I immediately got on the floor with her and was able to help her up. I took her hands and led her through some box breathing exercises, which immediately sent a calming response to her brain and gave her body a pause to get her breathing back to normal. We then did a visualization exercise, which enabled her to get her mind off of what triggered the panic attack and onto something more calming and endearing to her. I had her think of something amazing in her life. As soon as she thought of the fond memory, her body responded within a few seconds, bringing that memory from the back of the brain to the front of the brain. (I'll explain how to use both of these tools in Chapter 8.)

After a few minutes, she was fine and able to go back into the restaurant with her husband. We exchanged Facebook profiles because I mentioned that I wanted to send her some more tools to handle her anxiety so she could prevent or at least control situations like this. Shortly after, she sent me a message thanking me, as she felt I had "saved her life."

I share this story with you not because I feel I should be flying around with a cape like a superhero but rather to show you that you have control over your mind and body at all times. You can calm your body down through your mind. If your thoughts run away with you and your anxiety pushes you out of the driver's seat, you or someone who is with you can do the same exercises I did with her.

Chapter 6

Whatever We Expect, We Get

"The best way to predict your future is to create it."

—Abraham Lincoln

Yes, Abe, yes! Now, all we have to do is figure out how to create it, right?

I am a huge positive thinking/self-help/law of attraction junkie. I cannot get enough of it. I have read so many books, gone to so many seminars, and listened to so many podcasts, and I have found that the one constant message that all the big thought leaders agree on is that your life and the experiences in it all depend on your mindset. Joyce Meyer put it best when she said, "You cannot have a positive life and a negative mindset."[1] They just do not go together. It reminds me of the

---

1. Joyce Meyer, Battlefield of the Mind: Winning the Battle in Your Mind (Anderson, IN: Warner Faith, 2002).

expression in business, "You can either make excuses, or you can make money. But you can't do both."

So, how do you get that awesome life you so deserve? Expect it. It's that easy. This is referred to as the law of attraction or manifestation. Let's talk about some techniques for practicing these.

While I am not an expert on the law of attraction, I have used the technique long enough to vouch that it does work. In fact, the law of attraction is always working.

I remember the time I tried to disprove it. I had read a book that stated if you thought of something you wanted to see—for example, a yellow butterfly—you would, in fact, see a yellow butterfly in your travels. Right away, my skeptical brain took over, and I agreed to try this experiment. My son and I decided we wanted to see a truck. Not just any truck, however, but a *purple* truck. That's right. How many purple trucks have you seen? I have seen zero because, after all, who would drive a purple truck?

I chuckled, as I knew for sure I had just outsmarted the law of attraction. It was late afternoon when we decided on the purple truck, and we did not go out of the house the rest of that day. The next day, my family and I packed up our car and went down the shore for some fun and sun in Ocean City,

New Jersey. I looked at every single truck. Not a purple one to be found. As the day went on, I forgot about my mission. We left the beach after a fun day and packed up our car. That was when I heard my son say, "Mom, look!"

Parked across the street was a work truck with a mural painted on the side, and the main background color was . . . you guessed it. *Purple*!

Now, the things you attract won't necessarily be delivered to you the next day, like it was in that instance. (I should know because I have been waiting for this "I Am a Princess" thing to kick in since I was five.) The only "trick" to the law of attraction and manifesting everything you want is you have to believe it as though it is already here. The first crucial step in getting what you want is to first *decide* what you want. After you decide *what* you want, your brain then figures out *how* to get it. Once these desires are set, your mind and the universe go to work. Your job is only to believe that you have it already.

This is key: you have to believe in yourself. Believing in yourself is the first thing you must do to practice the law of attraction. You must believe you are worthy of the thing you want—and, therefore, the life you desire. One of the most powerful tools for building belief in yourself—and, therefore, obtaining the life you desire—is repeating positive statements, or affirmations. Now, I don't mean repeating them just a few times. I mean repeating them until they become a part of your everyday natural thought process. Over time, these positive affirmations will replace the negative thoughts in your subconscious. You have to visualize and feel what you want and act as though you already have it. Dress the part. Rather than saying, "I want to get a good job," you should say, "I *have* a good job." The universe needs to see that you are stepping into the good job you already have before the next one is delivered. You have to do the work. You will soon stop calling your manifestations coincidences and realize how powerful you are.

It's as the late, great Wayne Dyer said, "It's not 'I'll believe it when I see it,' it's 'I'll see it when I believe it.'" Instead, most people say, "I'll believe it when I see it."[2]

The universe notices things in real time and doesn't notice the negative connotation. For example, you would say, "I want to be on time," vs. "I don't want to be late." Or "I always have enough money" vs. "I don't want to be poor." Always use present tense with a positive connotation. Think of manifesting the things you want as easily as ordering something online. You go online, you find something you want to order, you press "Add to Cart," you put your payment in, and it is soon delivered to you. Easy! Well, manifesting is the same way. The universe is your online

---

2. Dr. Wayne W. Dyer, **You'll See It When You Believe It** (New York, NY: William Morrow and Co., 1989).

store. Except, rather than having to click on your item, you just say it aloud! There is no "Add to Cart." The universe heard you! And better yet, there is no payment. All you have to believe is that you have it. If you do that, it will be delivered to you! (More on affirmations in Chapter 7, "The Positivity Tool Kit.")

Remember, whatever you expect, that's what you are going to get. Whatever you are focusing on, whatever you are believing, that is what will be delivered to you. The Earth spins on energy. Everything is made up of energy. It only makes sense that what you throw out there comes right back at you like a boomerang. Some call this karma. Whatever you put out there will come right back to you, sometimes to bite you in the ass. So keep those affirmations, thoughts, words, and actions positive.

Most importantly, you have to believe in yourself. For example, Tony Robbins is one of my favorite personal growth coaches. He's six foot six, he's charismatic, and he commands his stage. If you have ever been to a Tony Robbins event, you can attest to the fact that he takes control of his audience. He jumps up and down and goes back and forth from one side of the stage to the other. He walks into the crowd, and his energy takes every listener over. It's an amazing experience! Tony has such a way of making people believe in themselves. His seminars show his audiences how to conquer limiting beliefs, face their fears, and develop a growth mindset, other things. An absolute high-energy experience!

Now, another one of my favorite motivational speakers is Nick Vujicic. Nick was born with tetra-amelia syndrome, which is the absence of all four limbs. Imagine if he gave himself that negative self-talk, compared himself to Tony Robbins, or didn't believe in himself or the gift he had to give. He would never be where he is today. He could very well have sat back like every single one of us and said, "Oh, I can't do that. I'm not Tony Robbins. I can't get up on that stage. He jumps up and down."

Obviously, Nick Vujicic cannot jump up and down. He cannot walk out into the crowd. He is not six foot six. He needs help with everything he does, yet he is one of the most powerful motivational speakers on the planet.

Why?

Because he has belief. He has the belief that he has something to give. He has the belief that he can make a difference. He had the belief that one day, he would have a beautiful wife and four children, and that's exactly what he has today. If you ever hear Nick Vujicic speak, you will walk away a different person, I promise you. He wanted to become a motivational speaker, so he manifested just that. He knew he had a gift that would help a countless number of people. He is simply amazing. All because he believed in himself.

One of my favorite demonstrations of belief is that of Russell Wilson and the Seattle Seahawks. Wilson was the quarterback for that team when they went to the Super Bowl in 2014. That year, they ended up winning the Lombardi trophy and the esteemed title of Super Bowl Champions. After the game, Wilson was being interviewed, and the reporter asked, "Russell, what have you been saying to your team all year as their leader to get them here and ultimately win the Super Bowl?" And his answer was simple. He said, "I just kept saying, 'Why not us?'" Exactly, Russell! Why not you? He poured into his team the belief that they were just as good as any other team in the NFL that year and that they could win the title of Super Bowl Champs. They believed they could, and they did.

You, too, can manifest whatever you want. All you have to do is get control of three things: the thoughts you think, the images you visualize, and the actions you take. To manifest something, first think about what you want. A new job? A new love interest? Then visualize it. If it is a job, visualize what your office looks like or perhaps the stage you want to speak on. Visualize the people you will be working with and the money you will make. If it is a love interest you want, visualize what they look like, how tall they are, how much they weigh, what color hair they have. Then believe it. Say it every day. Think about it and visualize it. Be as specific as you can.

You can be and have whatever you desire. All you have to do is believe. There are people less qualified than you who are doing the things you want to do.

Why?

Because they believe in themselves. Period. Life is not about who you once were. It's about who you are now and who you have the potential to be. You are not what has happened to you. You are what you choose to become. There will always be naysayers out there trying to keep you down. You cannot control what other people say or do. You can only control how you *react* to what other people say or do. You can control your own life, the belief you have in yourself, and, therefore, your destiny.

Attract what you expect, reflect what you desire, become who you respect, and be what you admire.

I mean really. Why not you?

Chapter 7

The Positivity Tool Kit

"A good tool improves the way you work. A great tool improves the way you think."

—Jeff Duntemann

Okay, so here we are! We have gotten to know each other. You now know what mindset is. You understand the importance of keeping it positive. And you know that just like you have to eat every day to make your body healthy, you have to learn every day to make your mind healthy. Surrounding yourself with tools that help you recondition your mind for success and positivity will ensure your growth and goal achievements. And you deserve that! There isn't a single person you require in this life more than yourself. Celebrate *you*. Put yourself first, and watch your life change.

In this chapter, I'm going to share some simple tools that will help you on your journey to becoming the best version of yourself. I have found that these tools have helped an endless number of people refocus and reframe their mindset. I encourage you to try them all. But, by all means, pick what works for you personally.

Journaling

Journaling is one of my favorite things to do. I will admit it takes a little while to become consistent with it, but once you are, it will absolutely keep you focused and disciplined. It has so many benefits and can be used for various reasons. There is something very therapeutic about taking a pen to paper and writing down the day's events, affirmations, future goals, manifestations, or even some stress-related thoughts that are renting space in your head. It is a fantastic way to release anger or sadness without the emotion festering. It also can aid in problem-solving, as seeing words on paper can help you absorb and better remember things. When you write things down, you tend to remember them longer. The art of repetition, baby! It never gets a chance to leave your mind, so all those positive ideas, thoughts, and goals stay with you until your actions become second nature and goal achievement becomes easier.

Journaling can also help with growth. Rereading past entries and reflecting can help you see how far you have come, even if the growth is not obvious to you. I can vouch firsthand that this is one of the most eye-opening exercises I have ever done. This is especially effective if you are not happy in your relationship—particularly if you are involved with a narcissist and/or in an abusive relationship. Writing down the day's events, your partner's mood, any triggers that set them off, and pertinent conversations will allow you to look back and remember the negative feelings they evoke. You might say, "Oh, how could anyone forget that?" Trust me, it's very easy. Narcissists and abusers have a way of being two different people, so when they are not abusing, they are kind and loving. Soon, you forget the awful things they said, the way they made you feel, and any hurtful actions (either physical or verbal) they took.

This is because the body's natural state is to be happy. For example, natural childbirth pains are one of the most intense physical pains a woman will ever feel. (Which is why I really love the inventor of the epidural, remember?) So why are they soon forgotten once the mother sees her beautiful child? Because the mind will choose happiness *every* time. Keeping a journal separates your emotions from the truth and allows you to maintain the facts so you can make whatever decision is necessary for not only your growth and positive mindset but, in some cases, your safety as well.

Finally, keeping a gratitude journal can lead to greater long-term happiness and more contentment in life overall. Gratitude journaling is a must for sustaining a positive mindset. Reflecting on the many things we are grateful for is a way to avoid slipping into the deep abyss of negativity when things don't go as we planned. And listen, you don't have to always be thankful for the big things, such as your family, your house, etc. (Although, by all means, write them down!) But start small, and look at the things that you take for granted every single day, such as your coffee, your bed, your shower with hot running water, the glass of water you are able to get right from your sink, the fact that you have a sink, etc. When you journal, these little things will open your eyes to all your blessings and create an attitude of gratitude that will soon become part of your daily mindset.

You can journal at any time of the day that works for you. Some people like to start their day off with journaling to kickstart their mindset. If you are just beginning your journaling journey, I suggest you do it at night, right before you go to bed. Write three things that you are grateful for from that day. Pick one from your morning, one from your afternoon, and one from your evening. That's it. No long dissertation is necessary. You are not presenting this to any board of directors. This is for you to reflect upon and be grateful.

Meditation

The practice of meditation is thousands of years old and has been proven to reduce stress, anxiety, and depression while promoting emotional health and overall well-being. Practicing meditation means deliberately focusing your attention to bring about calmness and self-awareness. You can achieve this by reciting a mantra (a sound, a word, or a group of words continually repeated during stillness), looking at an object, or doing intentional breathing exercises. While meditation is prominent among Buddhists, anyone can meditate. Don't worry—you do not have to shave your head, cover yourself in beads, and wear a robe resembling a burlap sack to enjoy meditation. You do not have to sit in the lotus position for hours on end either.

Meditation is usually practiced in a quiet space alone or in a group, where everyone is meditating. However, you can also do it walking, painting, fishing, or sitting on the beach. It is not about thinking of nothing, nor is it about asking for anything. It is about calming your mind and body and learning to be present, to rest in the here and now, fully engaged with whatever you are doing in the moment. Easier said than done. I remember that when I first started to meditate, I ended up mentally preparing my grocery list every week while I was learning to be present. But it is called a meditation "practice" for a reason. With practice, swarming thoughts soon started to leave, and, in my case, I am now able to get into my meditative state within minutes. According to several studies, twenty minutes of meditation a day for forty-five to sixty days can have measurable effects on the brain, ranging from better focus to less anxiety.

Prayer

Prayer allows a connection with God and, therefore, the feeling of being connected to a higher power that can provide guidance and clarity. It can be a means of seeking healing and forgiveness, which can allow for personal growth. Believers may feel less stress knowing they have a higher power in charge. Praying can contribute to feelings of tranquility, which inhibit the release of cortisol, therefore reducing the negative impact of stress. Prayer is usually a practice that believers do daily. I would say that if you are not a believer, then just "popping in" on God just because you need something might not elicit those warm and fuzzy feelings just described. But give it a go. God does amazing things.

I practice both prayer and meditation. I admit that I will take all the help I can get. I sometimes think that every time I do something stupid, God and Buddha look at each other and say, "I took care of her last time. It's your turn." I keep them pretty busy. I also think my spirit guide is often busy playing cards or something. Either that or they're just not talking loud enough for me to hear them. They are too busy rolling their eyes at me. Anyway, moving along . . .

Physical/Mental Swap

My dad used to say that when you are hurting mentally, do something physical, as physical activity releases the feel-good neurotransmitters called endorphins, which can aid in reducing stress or anxiety. Conversely, when you are hurting physically, do something mental, like working on a crossword puzzle or reading, as it will distract your brain from focusing on any discomfort or pain. This has worked wonders for me.

When I left my classroom marriage, it was the end of November 1999. I drove twelve hours home in a snowstorm and moved back in with my mom and dad at age thirty-eight. Listen, my mom and dad were the two best people on the planet, but let's be real here . . . talk about low self-esteem! My mindset was not stellar, to say the least.

After I got settled, I decided to start my Christmas baking and freeze all the goodies. I baked every single day from the middle of November to December 20. The physical activity of standing, stirring, kneading, cutting, decorating, and moving around the kitchen for hours took my mind off anything negative. When I took everything out of the freezer, I could not believe how many desserts I had! Actually, it was a ridiculous amount. It looked like Betty Crocker had blown up in my kitchen.

It was amazing how doing something physical (baking) eased my mind and helped me to stay out of the "poor me" zone while processing the major changes happening in my life. I gained five pounds that Christmas season. But on the positive side, I was emotionally stable!

Box Breathing

Breath work is a great way to calm the central nervous system and reduce stress. I do box breathing, as I find it reduces anxiety and improves mood. It can help you cope with panic and stress when you're feeling overwhelmed, which is exactly what it did in the story I shared in Chapter 4. It immediately sends a calming response to the brain and gives your body a pause.

There are many ways to do box breathing. I do a four-count breath.

Step 1: Breathe in slowly through your nose for a count of four. Feel the air enter your lungs.

Step 2: Hold for a count of four. Try to avoid inhaling or exhaling for four seconds.

Step 3: Release for a count of four, slowly exhaling through your mouth.

Step 4: Hold for a count of four.

Repeat three times or until you feel centered. This type of breathing exercise can be done anytime and anywhere—even while driving.

Visualization

Visualization exercises are extremely effective for reframing your mindset. When talking about mindset, I tell whomever I am speaking to that I will show them how their thoughts can affect their emotions, all within a minute. This is to prove to them that they control their mindset and, therefore, control their emotions.

First, I have them all think of the saddest memory they can think of—a death, a loss, an argument, or anything that makes them incredibly sad. I have them think heavily on that thought for seventeen seconds. (Now, while I have been doing this exercise for quite some time, I got the seventeen seconds from the incredible Esther Hicks, who claims it takes only seventeen seconds for you to set in motion a chain reaction of either negative or positive energy, depending on what your thought is.)

After those seventeen seconds, I have them open their eyes and tell me how they are feeling. Of course, from their body language, I can already tell how they feel. There are no smiles. They are not sitting up straight. They are looking around the room, probably thinking, *Gee. Thanks, Beth. Who the hell invited you anyway?*

But I then quickly have them do the same thing again for seventeen seconds, only this time with a positive, fun, or funny memory. I tell them to think of something that immediately makes them smile or even laugh when it comes to mind. It could be their wedding day, the birth of their child, the day they got their puppy, or anything that brings them joy or makes them laugh. Again, I have them concentrate on this thought for seventeen seconds.

When they open their eyes after these seventeen seconds, the energy in the room is completely different. There are smiles and laughter, and the body language is completely open. The difference in their energy between the first thought and the second thought is staggering. They literally changed their energy with their thoughts. And it took only seventeen seconds! I did nothing but hold the stopwatch. They were in control of their thoughts and, therefore, their energy.

It is important to note that thinking of an actual memory is faster and more powerful than thinking of something imaginary, such as a beautiful scene. People relate to their own experiences faster and with more feeling. Just like meditation, you will find that with practice, this becomes increasingly easier to manipulate. You will know the exact thought that will uplift you and put you in a better mood. And the beauty of it is that it is your very own positive thought!

Affirmations

Affirmations, such as "I am" statements, are important for reframing your mindset. The more you practice your positive affirmations, the more your brain aligns with what you are reciting. The art of repetition is so powerful. Affirmations mold your mindset to navigate toward your goals. As stated previously, affirmations ("I am" statements) should always be positive and have a positive connotation.

As a motivational speaker, every time my dad stepped on stage to speak, he would ask the audience to stand. He would then have them recite, together as a crowd, "I'm happy, I'm healthy, and I feel good!" They would do this three times before sitting back down.

There was definitely a method to his madness. Happiness and positive emotions, similar to the ones evoked by positive affirmations, increase your information and processing skills and help you memorize new material. Since Daddio was a sales trainer, he wanted his audience to remember the skills and information he was presenting.

Affirmations can be tailor made to whatever you are seeking to achieve. Here are a few to get started with every morning.

- I am having a great day.
- I am making the right choices.
- I have inner strength.
- I radiate positive energy.
- I am perfect just the way I am.

Remember, results come from believing affirmations, not just from saying them. You can recite positive affirmations and even put them on a Post-it note on your mirror. But if you are following them up with thoughts of disbelief that it will ever come to fruition, guess what? It's not going to come to fruition. Negative self-talk is so powerful that it will always win. Every. Damn. Time. Pour belief into those affirmations so that negative self-talk can't rear its ugly head.

Here is a list of affirmations depending on your goal.

You Have Courage:

"I am a courageous person. I have the courage to stand up for myself. I see change as an opportunity to grow."

You Are a Happy Person:

"I have a positive outlook in life. Every day, I am grateful for my life. I am always happy."

You Love Yourself:

"I love myself for who I am as a person. I appreciate all the good qualities I have. I enjoy my own company."

You Are Optimistic:

"My internal voice is optimistic at all times. I have a naturally positive internal dialogue. I believe in myself deeply."

You Have Strong Beliefs about Money:

"I am good with money and naturally seek it out. I am making more money now than ever before. I am entitled to be rich."

You Have a Millionaire Mindset:

"I deserve to make a million dollars. I thrive under pressure. I am a millionaire."

You Are Confident:

"I am very self-confident. I believe in myself and know I can do anything I put my mind to. I effortlessly converse with other people."

You Can Lose Weight:

"I burn calories quickly. I only eat healthy food. Every day, I am getting slimmer."

You Are Productive:

"I get things done within my target time. I am a productive, motivated, and highly driven person. I naturally get things done and take action when required."

You Have Attracted Your Soulmate:

"My soulmate is getting closer. I am destined to meet my soulmate. My perfect partner is just around the corner."

You Attract Success:

"I am attracting success in my life. I rise to any challenge that comes my way. I can and will achieve all of my dreams."

You Live the Law of Attraction:

"The law of attraction is working for me every day. I have the power to attract whatever I want in life. I am always attracting abundance in my life."

You Are a Positive Thinker:

"I am a positive person. I can do anything I set my mind to. My future is looking brighter and brighter."

Reading/Podcasts

Reading ten pages a day of a book from a thought leader on positive energy and self-improvement is crucial for maintaining a positive mindset. Listening to podcasts or audiobooks is just as effective. Not only are you learning, but a daily dose of positive messages will train your brain to find solutions instead of obstacles should they arise. When you read something positive or repeat affirmations, for example, you allow your subconscious mind to absorb new information. Eventually, your conscious mind will accept the information as fact and a new belief. And a new positive belief is born.

I love to read. There is something about turning the pages of a book that gives me a sense of accomplishment. However, when I am driving, it is difficult to hold a book *and* drink my coffee *and* put my mascara on at the same time, so I opt for podcasts or audiobooks. My car becomes a rolling university, especially on long trips. Whatever way your brain best absorbs knowledge is good. There is no right or wrong way. Just get the information in, process it, and watch your life change.

It is important to note that you can use any of the above tools at any time of the day. In saying that, I find it most effective if positivity practices are done first thing in the morning and/or right before bedtime. Starting your day with a good mindset is invaluable, while what your brain absorbs prior to falling asleep is significantly responsible for how you wake up. When you fall asleep, your conscious mind shuts down, and your subconscious takes over. When you awaken, your conscious mind takes over again and picks up where it left off. If you are negative before bed, watch horror movies, or watch graphic, violent shows before you fall asleep, not only will you not get a good night's sleep, but you will probably wake up feeling out of balance.

Here is a list of just some of my favorite books:

Real Magic by Wayne W. Dyer

You Can Heal Your Life by Louise Hay

One Day My Soul Just Opened Up by Iyanla Vanzant

Don't Sweat the Small Stuff by Richard Carlson, PH.D

Super Attractor by Gabrielle Bernstein

Ask and It is Given by Esther and Jerry Hicks

You Are a Badass by Jen Sincero

Mindset Matters Most by Brian J. Grasso

The Five Second Rule by Mel Robbins

For free Breath Work and Visualization exercises go to my Instagram @funnyysister

Chapter 8

Embrace Your Season

"My mission in life is not merely to survive but to thrive, and to do so with some passion, some compassion, some humor and some style."

—Maya Angelou

If you have reached this point of the book, you are now equipped with some tools, coping skills, and, most of all, confidence to be who you are meant to be without apologies, regret, or fear.

As human beings, we need to stay watered in order to grow. And, most importantly, we need to embrace each season we are in, not fear it. Embrace where you are right now. If you find yourself depressed, you are living in the past. If you find yourself anxious or have a sense of fear, you are living in the future. Be right here right now.

We all have seasons. Just as you embrace each season of the year, you must learn to embrace each season of your life. For example, I love autumn. Yoga pants, pumpkin spice lattes, football, hoodies, Halloween, my birthday, and more! However, many people have a difficult time transitioning from the summer season to the fall season. Why is this? Well, for one, we are moving out of the long, high-energy summer days to shorter, darker days, cooler weather, and a general downshift in the cycle of life. During the warm months, we spend so much time outside that we get a sufficient amount of vitamin D from the sun. Sunshine boosts the body's level of serotonin, which improves mood and helps us stay calm and focused. Also, we have outdoor treats in the summertime. Ice cream and other sugary sweets release dopamine, which is a neurotransmitter that works in conjunction with serotonin to increase pleasure and joy. It makes us happy, even if it's just a quick fix.

However, when autumn does arrive, we don't say, "Oh, wait. But I'm mentally still in summer, so I am going to wear my bathing suit even though it is fifty degrees outside." No, we transition and embrace the fall season! We wear boots, we go to football games, we might do indoor projects. Whatever it is, we adapt and do fall activities.

Well, it's the same with your personal life seasons. You must learn to move through these cycles too. I realize it may not always be an easy task. There absolutely are better life seasons than others, but even in the not-so-good seasons, you get through! It doesn't have to be difficult; however, many people struggle to find happiness with where they are. When we are young, we want to be older. When we are older, we want to be younger. When we look good, we think we are fat. When we put on weight, we wish we were as "fat" as we were when we thought we were fat. It's exhausting!

The struggle could be in part due to the fact that people are trying to live their lives according to what and how society says they should. Society will have you believing you should get married at a certain age, have children by a certain age, and buy a house by a certain age. The list goes on and on.

It is all bullshit. Live life according to you. Your journey is completely different from someone else's journey. There are so many different seasons. Becoming a mother, becoming a mother-in-law, becoming an empty nester, changing jobs, experiencing hormonal changes, getting married, getting divorced—the list goes on and on. And with each new season comes something new, something unknown. You may find yourself struggling to navigate this new season because you managed life in the last season so effortlessly. I am here to tell you that is normal. Every bit of it. The unsureness, the fear of stepping out of your comfort zone, the what-ifs.

However, as you enter each new season of your life, there are some things you can do to stay focused and confident.

1. Be present.

Whether it is a high season or a low season, being present will help you stay focused. It allows you to see your situation better, therefore equipping you with the proper tools to adjust, thrive in, and enjoy the time you are in that season.

2. Set new personal goals.

New goals are crucial for adapting to a new season. While some things may stay the same, some are bound to change. You may have more free time. You may want to change your diet. Whatever it is, write down your goals so they are visible to you. It helps to keep you on track.

3. Join a group.

Whether you have just gone through a divorce or are now an empty nester looking to meet new people, groups are a great way to connect with others. If it is a support group or just a networking group you seek, getting yourself into one can help with your seasonal transition.

4. Focus on the positives.

When transitioning to a new season, especially a low season, it is imperative that you stay focused on the positives. A low season may make you feel as though there are no positives, but I assure you there are. Staying centered on the good points of your season will decrease stress and allow you to move forward.

5. Determine what is working.

Each season is different, and what may have worked in your last season may not work in this one. Last season's behaviors, people, or actions may not work in your new season. Determine what works and what must change. Recognize your progress.

6. Practice self-care.

Whatever that may mean to you. Meditate, pray, get massages, be alone, be with people, get a manicure, go out to dinner—whatever works for you! It is your journey. It is your season.

Make it easy on yourself, and embrace each season that you are in. It could be a season of growth in your mindset. Perhaps a season of just getting older. A season of changing your workout. I have a couple of dear friends who were female bodybuilders, and now that they have come to a certain age, they cannot lift such heavy weights anymore. So they have embraced the season, and they now do different forms of movement, such as yoga and Pilates. When my son was in school playing baseball, I would tell him that champions are made in the offseason. It is during those difficult seasons of storms that the growth happens.

In these low seasons, it is particularly important to protect your energy and your mindset. You never want to make a negative decision in the low time, and you certainly never want to make your most important decisions when you are in your worst moods. You want to wait. Be patient. The storm will pass. Your spring will come with new life and new possibilities.

The most important thing to remember when you are going through different seasons of life is that people may quit on you, and that's okay. Just make sure you do not ever quit on yourself. Keep moving. Embrace the season—get watered and grow! And do not compare yourself to others. Not everyone handles the same season in the same way. I remember when my friend and I both received AARP information in the mail. American Association for Retired Persons (AARP) sends out information when a person turns fifty years old and, for a small membership fee, gives discounts on travel, insurance, movies, etc. My friend immediately threw it away as she thought it meant she was old. She wanted nothing to do with it. I, on the other hand, said, "Oh good, I reached the age where people are giving me stuff! I love it! What do I get!?"

As I stated in Chapter 1, always remind yourself that your track record for making it through your bad days is perfect. It's 100 percent! You are better than you think. Do whatever works for you in your season. Each life season provides different lessons and new areas for growth. Every step, every challenge, and every moment has brought you to this point. It's all part of your unique path to grow into who you are supposed to be. Embracing each new life season and knowing that each one is fleeting will help you move through your cycles with positivity and grace. Grow through what you go through. The task ahead of you is never greater than the strength within you.

Most importantly, do not be hard on yourself. It is the small habits that will help. How you spend your mornings, how you talk to yourself, what you read, what you watch, who you share your energy with, and who has access to you will change your life. It will all help you embrace whatever season you find yourself in.

Love *where* you are. Love *who* you are. Being happy is a self-responsibility. Another human cannot fulfill that for you. Life is not about who you once were. It is about who you are now and who you have the potential to be.

Don't be afraid to start over. Remember that you are not starting from scratch. This time, you are starting from experience. Something will grow from all that you are going through. And it will be you. So go do some main character shit before it's too late!

The end result is happiness, self-love, being the best person you can be, controlling the things you can control, and, most of all, learning to laugh.

Because, after all, laughter is an instant vacation.

Here's What to Do Next

It's bigger than a book!

Whenever you're ready, here are four ways we can help you take the next step on your book journey:

1. Access all your free breathwork and visualization exercises on Instagram at @funnyysister

2. Contact me to be your mindset mentor. I'd love to chat with you. Email bdodd1102@gmail.com to schedule a call with "MINDSET" in the subject line.

3. Hire Beth to Speak

If you are looking for a high-energy motivational speaker for your conference, event, or mastermind, I'd love to bring it! A little laughter mixed with mindset tools never hurt anyone!

Email bdodd1102@gmail.com with "SPEAKING" in the subject line.

4. Connect on Social Media

Let's keep the convo going! The journey doesn't end here. I'd love to connect with you on all social platforms. Let's have some fun!

You can find me on social at @funnyysister

Acknowledgments

To my mom, Bette, my dad, Bob, my sister, Barbie, and my brother, Bobby. Thank you all for giving me the absolute best childhood and for molding me into the person I am today. Mom and Dad, thank you for giving me what I consider to be your strongest assets:

Mom—Your strong sense of self, your "Don't take shit from anyone" attitude, your amazing skills as a mother, and your ability to be strong on the outside yet kind on the inside. I am proud to be like you. You were my best friend who knew everything about me and liked me anyway. I hope you hear me talking to you because I often do.

Dad—Your positivity, sense of humor, and kind heart were second to none. I wrote this book not just *for* you but *because of* you. I have learned so much from you over the years, and I use what you taught me every single day. Your love for mankind and genuine appreciation for life is unmatched to this day. Your ability to make even the toughest times bearable was a gift from God. And so were you, Daddio. You were the best.

I miss you both immensely.

Barbie and Bobby—Thank you for being the best older siblings ever, from watching out for me as a child to becoming the keepers of my secrets. You both have qualities I only wish I could have. I have admired you both for a lifetime. You have given me more credit than I deserved at times, and it has never gone unnoticed. Also, thank you for being born before me and doing all the mischievous things teenagers do. This allowed me to do the same things except *not* get caught like you did. Being the youngest rocks! Love you both.

To my extended family and my friends— How lucky am I that I can put you in the same category! My extended family are my friends, and my friends are my family. Thank you for the laughs, the fun, the talks, the lessons, and most of all the love. Thank you for always being willing to ride down that one-way road of life with me . . . going the opposite way of course! The memories that I have over the years always manage to bring laughter to my heart. I look forward to making many more with you all.

To Bola Adelakun, a.k.a. "Bola A"—You went from my employer to my mentor and my friend. Thank you for allowing me to bust into your office at any given time to discuss my challenge of the week, or even sometimes my challenge of the day! Thank you for always putting things in perspective for me with your wise words. You have never been too busy to listen. Thank you for believing in me and this book, and for pouring that belief into my cup on the days when it was empty. Most importantly, thank you for accepting my cursing and shitty computer skills. (Oops, sorry. That slipped out.) You are an incredible person, and I cannot wait for you to be on that speaking stage so the world can see the gift that is you.

To Jake Kelfer and the staff at Big Idea to Bestseller— Thank you all for helping make this book possible, especially Adrienne, who took all the mumbled, jumbled information in my head and helped me sort it out and make it all make sense, and Mikey, who kept my non-focused mind straight. Your patience was unwavering, and I hold so much appreciation for you. And a big thank-you to editors Ashton and Catt Editing LLC for their suggestions and keen eyes!

And now, I saved the best for last—my grand finale:

To my family:

Steve, my other half. I don't know where I would be if you hadn't come into my life when you did. Thank you for always accepting me for who I am—the good, the bad, and the ugly. Thank you for always loving me and caring about me, and never being afraid to show it. Thank you for laughing at my silly jokes, even when you were the brunt of them or (dare I say) even if they weren't funny. Thank you for going on this journey of life with me and never jumping off! To our kids Stephen, Neil, and Nicholas. The joy I have in my heart having watched you all grow into the amazing men you are supersedes all else. Thank you for putting up with my craziness and accepting it all as the norm. I am so proud of each one of you. My family, I could never find the words to express how much you have individually and collectively changed my life for the better. I am forever grateful. And a special thank-you to my beautiful daughters-in-law for jumping on this crazy train with us and sharing all your love and laughter! I love you all xo

Hey there, reader! If you enjoyed this book, I would be forever grateful if you could take a moment to leave a review on Amazon. Think of it as your good deed for the day, like helping an old lady cross the street or not eating the last cookie. Plus, it helps other readers find this book. So go ahead, click those stars and type some kind words (or funny emojis), and make my day!

About the Author

In addition to being an author, mindset mentor, and mental health professional, Beth Dodd is just a girl from Jersey—a Scorpio at that. This means, among other things, she's passionate about what she believes in, and family is everything. She credits her dad for her humor and positivity, and her mother for her toughness on the exterior and softness on the inside. All of this Beth brings into her work mentoring people through life's biggest challenges. As she shares in her book, "No matter how bad a situation is, there is always light at the end of a tunnel, and I promise you it is not an oncoming train."

Beth wrote *Laughter Is an Instant Vacation* to share her life experiences and the coping skills she has learned along the way. There's no such thing as a lifetime without clouds, but Beth is here to reassure you that with the right tools, a different mindset, and a little bit of laughter, the sun will come out again.

Made in the USA
Middletown, DE
21 September 2024

61078818R00081